I Am A Woman,
I Am A God

For My Friend
Carolyn

♡

I Am A Woman, I Am A God

Louise Oliverio

To order additional copies of this book, contact:
Xlibris Corporation
1-888-795-4274
www.Xlibris.com
Orders@Xlibris.com
35316

Permissions

I wish to extend my appreciation to the authors and publishers for granting me permission to use their works which are quoted in this book—Louise Oliverio

For more information about Ramtha's teachings contact: Ramtha's School of Englightenment, a division of JZK, Inc., P.O. Box 1210, Yelm, WA 98597, USA. www.ramtha.com.

Culture of Life Foundation, Washington, DC.

The Complete Bill of Rights, The Drafts, Debates, Sources, & Origins, Edited by Neil H. Cogan, Vice President and Dean, Whittier Law School

Excerpts from: Ken Wilber, author—The Spectrum of Consciousness—Fifth Quest Book Printing 1989

Dr. Stephan A. Hoeller, author—Jung and The Lost Gospels—Third Quest Printing 1993

Reprinted by permission of Quest Books/The Theosophical Publishing House, Wheaton, Ill. (www.questbooks.net).

A Course in Miracles, Foundation for Inner Peace—1975

Doug Craigen, a former Acadia University physics professor—www.dctech.com.

Colummist, Mort Crim—Mort Crim Communications, Inc., article "Keeping It" 2004

American Society of Plastic Surgeons, Arlington Heights, IL 60005—Report 2002 Statistics, Released: April 15, 2003

About the Author

My journey began in the 1970's after reading books by Ruth Montgomery regarding reincarnation. I became involved in metaphysics which included taking courses by various educators in the art of Therapeutic Touch and Reiki Healing with the beginning understanding of our electromagnetic field and healing processes using the power within us.

In the mid 1980's, I began studying under Ramtha, the entity who JZ Knight channels. During this time, I have studied various subjects in areas of theology, philosophy, consciousness, quantum physics and other branches of science.

I live in Yelm, Washington where I continue my studies with Ramtha. I have been taught the unlimited potentials of our mind, including fundamental concepts and disciplines of, *The Nature of Consciousness and Energy, What Is Destiny? Who Is Responsible for Personal Destiny? Can It Be Changed?, Study of the Chemistry and Function of the Brain in the Creation of Reality, Ability to Physically Heal Yourself and Others,* plus much more. I experienced these and other phenomenon. Studying these subjects necessitates the understanding of oneself, how we think, including what one's true beliefs are. The experience and realizations becomes one's truth. My truth is what I share within these pages.

Contents

Thank You

To those friends who have encouraged me to bring
this information to all who desire it, along with a very
special thanks to my dear friend Paula Maislen.

Acknowledgment

I first and foremost give my thanks and appreciation to the God within me that has given me the reality of the creation of these words.

Without Ramtha, JZ Knight and Ramtha School of Enlightenment, I may never in this lifetime remembered who I am or had the experience of it.

My beautiful children, who are also on the path and their families, Natalie Oliverio, Audra Oliverio Sheedy, Jennifer Oliverio, Grandchildren Bella, Ariel Temra, Ryan and Juliana.

To my beautiful family who, by love always allowed me my freedom, to act, think, be and experience without the stronghold of family and cultural ties of control.

Chapter 1

I am a Woman, I am a God

For many years I have known that God is within me, that I am a God. I thought I believed it. What I didn't know was that there was an attitude in me, which really didn't believe it. The understanding of that came after many years of study in Ramtha's School of Ancient Wisdom. I came to understand my ignorance in that, somewhere in my subconscious mind, I really thought only a man could be God. Why wouldn't I think that, after all it is what women have always been taught? In all the religions, who is God? A man of course!—Well teaching the word of God couldn't come from a woman because too—man—is the representative of God. Isn't he?? Oh! and what about those Gurus—men too aren't they? Popes, Priests, Rabbis, etc. Well, where do women fit in the scheme of things? Are we to be forever subservient to God and man? I think that was the plan. But wait a minute. Who made that plan God or man? Well let's see, as far as I know, God created man in his image. What image was that? Human? Spirit? What? I say that because if God was in the beginning, where and when nothing else existed, then what represents God's image? Is it human form? Is it man not woman? Is it woman not man? What was his image anyway?

I was brought up in the Catholic Religion. The neighborhood or area in which I lived was a place where most of the residents practiced the Jewish Religion. In both religions, man was the go between you and God and God was a man. Priests for example were God's emissaries. Nuns were their helpers. The priests were closer to God than the nuns. You spoke to the priest confessing any sins you were thought to have committed, according to the religious doctrines. The priest in turn forgave you on behalf of God or spoke to God on your behalf asking God to forgive you. In those days, one was not allowed to simply forgive oneself, we just weren't taught that. After all, the priests knew better than you since they studied the Bible, the so-called word of God or should I say the ONLY word of God, as was taught. The only thing anyone else had to think about was making sure you went to church on Sunday, followed the rituals and went to confession to confess your sins. The Ten Commandments written in the Bible were the moral rules to adhere to and if you didn't, well you sinned against God and probably would be punished in some way. There were also sins if you didn't follow some, if not all, of the rituals the church dreamed up for you.

In my early years, women couldn't enter church to participate in a mass unless they wore a hat to cover their heads, I suspect, lest their beautiful hair be exposed to entice man or man priest causing them to sin or have sinful thoughts—as if that would stop it. A woman's hair was always treasured by her for that was considered her crown of beauty. Women also could not bare their shoulders and had to wear short sleeves or long sleeves. Even the poor nuns had to wear black robes, shave their hair and wear ritual headpieces. The nuns were subservient to the priests. There was even a time long ago, when women couldn't receive communion. They were not considered good enough to receive the "sacrament" of holy communion represented by a wafer. What a state of affairs.

As far as I know of the Jewish Religion, women were not Rabbis and were not allowed to study the Hebrew texts (remember the movie Yentle, starring Barbra Streisand?). This movie may not have been entirely factual but it did bring out the inequities facing women in that religion also. In fact, in the old testaments, if you read them, God was particularly partial to men. Only men were allowed to wear the special robes of God and walk with the Ark of the Covenant. Women were severely punished for the slightest of discretions. Where does mercy come in? What about the Ten commandments? All these questions? Who is there to answer them? The men seemed to have all the power, all the advantages. They wield an enormous amount of power over women. The men had harems and did basically anything they wished to do. The women were always less, even considered soulless, if you will.

Even today in various countries women are treated as little more than dogs. Women are not allowed to show the slightest amount of skin lest they tempt man. Someone has to be blamed for the men's sins. They don't want to suffer for their own thoughts and deeds. They may never get to heaven. The women's private parts mutilated, as in Afghanistan, so as not even to have the pleasure that the man keeps for himself. It seems that in China there has been an edict whereby citizens may only have one child. The citizens are asked to abort fetuses, especially if the fetus is a girl and be sterilized afterwards.

> Mass Infanticide in China Posted by the Culture of Life Foundation—China—"Two researchers say comprehensive new data shows that traditional family patterns in China, combined with tough population-control measures, have resulted in "female infanticide on a grand scale"—close to 800,000 baby girls abandoned or killed in a single region between 1971-80 alone. G. William Skinner, an anthropologist and China specialist at the University of California-Davis, and Chinese researcher Yuan Jianhua based their conclusions on an analysis of 1990 Chinese census data. They presented their findings at the Association for Asian Studies' annual meeting last weekend in San Diego. While the phenomenon of disappearing girls isn't new, the paper by Yuan and Skinner is the first to show how location and family composition help determine infants' fate: The more rural a baby girl's surroundings, and the more sisters she had at birth, the higher her chances of not surviving. The researchers say most of the girls were abandoned or killed at birth. Chinese officials have long maintained that missing girls are adopted or raised on the sly, but Skinner said the data does not allow for concealment."

What a travesty of human rights against women but the biggest travesty of human rights I see against women has been the separation of women from God. This has been perpetrated upon them for eons.

No matter what the differences are between humans, all men were created equal. I think that should have been changed to all men and women or all humans are created equal. Leaving the specific word women out of the equation continues to keep them separated and less than men as if God only created men equally, then women were created but not equal to men. Case in point.

> The Complete Bill of Rights, The Drafts, Debates, Sources, & Origins, Edited by Neil H. Cogan, on page 349, 10.1.3.1 Connecticut, 10.1.3.1.b Declaration of Rights, 1776 states: "[2] And be it further Enacted and Declared, by the Authority aforesaid, That *no Man's Life* shall be taken away: *No Man's Honor* or good Name shall be stained: *No Man's Person* shall be arrested, restrained, banished, dismembered, nor any ways punished: *No Man shall be deprived of his Wife* or Children: *No Mans' Goods or Estate* shall be taken away from him, nor any ways indamaged under the colour of Law, or countenance of Authority; unless clearly warranted by the laws of this State." (Emphasis added).

If one looks at that it seems to cover every aspect of one's possessions, Name, Honor Goods, Estates, Wife, etc. Wife being the relevant word here because that would lead one to believe that the Bill of Rights only applied to men and not women otherwise it may have said, no man or woman instead of only the word man. They would have left the word wife out, because it wouldn't have been necessary to indicate "wife" or simply have said "No Man's or Woman's Honor or good Name", etc. To me the above denotes the thinking at the time and still in today's world. Lucky for women the words, later on, every person, or subject or citizen, inhabitant etc. were also used which, it is thought, includes women in those meanings. Even in that, women were not given the right to vote until the 1900's. Weren't we all supposed to be equal under the laws of God and men? Didn't we, as women have the same rights as men from the beginning? Why would we need an Equal Rights Amendment, when under the Constitution of the United States, everyone, including women supposedly already had those rights, including the right to vote? Why did women have to fight for that????

If you look at the human and spiritual qualities of male and female, one of the first things you will notice is the light in their eyes, that special sparkle when they are happy and the change when they are sad. Someone said, the eyes are the windows of the soul. Would that then mean that women have souls too? Well everything else apparently is the same, we each have blood running through our veins, skin, various organs, beating heart etc. etc. Aside from the differences relating to procreation, where is the difference? If there is no difference, then why do you suppose that, if it is true that God made man in his own image, that wouldn't apply to women also? I think that people generally think, when speaking of God's image, that one would be referring to the human image. If the image were a human (I don't personally think that is a correct understanding) wouldn't it also apply to women with regards to being equal to men?

Perhaps God's own image wasn't human but etheric in nature, that it is the essence of God, the breath of life breathed into human form and in fact, every form. In the beginning God was, then came everything else. Of what did God create everything else—night and day, stars, moons, all the cosmos, air, trees, birds, creatures of all sorts? If God was all that was, then out of what was God created? It is my understanding God created everything from the energy that God itself is. All things then, including humans, being a part of God itself have all the qualities/traits/power of God. As in procreation, the egg and the sperm developing and out of the two comes the newborn. The newborn has the qualities of both parents. In the same way, everything, including humans, have the qualities of God. Any separation whatsoever is impossible just as it would be impossible to separate the qualities of both parents from a newborn. The children inherit all the human qualities/traits, therefore, the child is just like the father, mother,—human.

Given the above, one would come to the conclusion that the qualities of God are also inherent in women and that women are not separate from God nor is man or any human. We are all Gods.

> John 10:34 "34 Jesus answered them," Is it not written in
> your Law, 'I have said you are gods'[5]?

Jesus didn't specify only men were Gods " . . . . you are gods". In other areas of the Bible, it is also written that the gods intercoursed with the women of men. Why were those people called "gods" small "g"? Who were they? What was the difference between the "gods", "women of men" and "God", capital "G". At the time some people were certainly considered gods. It is my understanding that we all are gods. How did our understanding of this change over time?

Women in ancient times were the oracles, (i.e.Druid Tradition) the Priestesses. Taken from The Golden Thread, June/July, 2001 magazine referencing The Bloodline of the Holy Grail, by Sir Laurence Gardner, it is said that:

> "The Grail in its chalice representation is a female symbol called the vasuterus, or womb. However, although the ancient Grail ceremony has been perpetuated in the Christian Eucharist sacrament, women have long been excluded from the priesthood. But this was not the case in Bible times, nor even in the Bible text. Indeed the Gospels themselves explain that Mary Magdalene was a priestess, while her marriage to Jesus is described in specific detail."
> " . . . It is really a question of reading what is written rather than listening to what is taught." "To understand the root of the laws and customs which applied in the Gospel era, it is necessary to step back again in time to see how and why those laws were contrived. In doing this (with the aid of firsthand documentary evidence) we can see that so much of what became religious dogma was born out of fear—hence the expression 'God fearing'. In an attempt to forge male dominated society from the time of Moses, such important figures as the once venerated wives of Jehovah were forsaken and this led to a loss of the earthly female ethic which caused no end of insurmountable problems for the generations to follow, even down to date"

The womb was considered sacred in those ancient times before women's fall, perhaps because that is where creation begins in bringing forth children. I think the ability to create another human(s) really is a sacred Godly act. Being Gods, we have the capacity to create as God did in the beginning, from ourselves including all the attributes of God.

If all of this is true then how is it that we have been so misled so as to think that God is a man, in particular one man instead of all humans, including women? Perhaps the foregoing, again taken from The Golden Thread, June/July, 2001, page 47 as above stated, had a lot to do with it.

> "The Roman Church condemned the red capped priestesses of the Grail Church as being 'scarlet women', proclaiming

them to be whores and witches. Even Jesus's mother Mary was not allowed to wear ecclesiastical colours in authorized artwork. But, in fact, it was the scarlet women who ran the schools and ministries of the original Jesus movement, in the company of those such as Lazarus and Joseph of Arimathea. In contrast, Peter and Paul are on record in the Vatican Constitutions as saying that women should 'be in silence' for they are not worthy of the Church!" (Emphasis added).

One of the hardest things I had to overcome in being a free willed, self empowered woman, was how a woman could be God. God is a man, in particular Jesus.

In Ramtha's School of Enlightenment, Ancient School of Wisdom, Yelm, Washington, which I have attended for 20 or so years, I have come to realize that one of the greatest obstacles to creating my own destiny is the belief that only a man is God. Through knowledge and experience, I realized that that attitude has been in my brain's neuro net, from childhood, in my cellular and genetic memory passed down through the ages. After all, I was brought up to believe, know, understand that a woman's place was in the home. The husband ruled the roost. Everything in my life was supposed to surround the husband's needs, wants, desires, the children's wants, needs and desires, the relatives' wants, needs and desires, the family rituals, those church rituals, etc. etc. God was a man. The "God", the "man", could and did punish. That was the programming for me and most other women.

In this school, however, we are taught that God is all things, this includes humans, all humans. That being the case, then it stands to reason that all of us would have the same attributes as God which includes the art of creation: creating songs, books, inventions, reality in people, places, things, times and events. If one thinks about it, every aspect of our lives are our creations created by our actions or inactions, choices, needs, dreams including most of all personal attitudes.

Everything in nature creates. The plants grow and die and grow again. The birds procreate. All breathing living entities procreate some way or another. Is this not creation? With humans though, we have something special, we have thought. With thought comes the ability to purposely create. We do create from our thoughts, which then bring on our emotions together with our inherent character/

personality that allows us to make certain choices in our lives. The choices we make are the roads we then experience. We experience the outcome (consequences) of those choices we make. We may not always like the experience but we always had a choice. Isn't that God like? Women are not excluded from this either.

Some women may think that their lives are pretty much destined for them but then that is excluding free will, which we all have, the free will of making choices and dreaming dreams. Those choices we make can be easy to follow or hard to follow meaning that we may suffer the consequences of a choice which we may feel is too much to overcome. Getting out of tight situations is always hard to overcome but we can and many do. The point is that women too have the capacity to create as a God with the freedom of mind to dream and until we look deep into our souls to see what or who we really understand God to be, we may not know what is standing in the way of our own evolvement and creative abilities. I am including men in this statement as well.

There are so many subtle attitudes women have regarding their true nature. These subtle attitudes come from many sources, as mentioned above, genetic, cellular memory, childhood experiences, movies, music, and probably most of all their religious persuasion. All of this is retained in the brain's neuro net which fires a memory or associative memory whenever we experience something, through our senses, such as, we may smell a particular flower, which would then remind us of an earlier experience. If the experience is a pleasant one then we react with joy. When the memory isn't pleasant then we react with sadness. In this way, we affect the environment around us. We can make a choice as to whether or not to continue to feel a certain way. We weren't taught we have the ability to create our own reality or to feel worthy of that reality or that we have the ability to change how we feel.

If we are victims in and of our realities, then we may very well choose to cry or be depressed. This would then satisfy the perhaps unknown desire to be an alone victim. We make these types of choices all the time. We do have a choice as to whether or not we will experience the smiles of the world or be alone. Most of our choices depend on how we truly feel about ourselves relating to self-worth, self confidence, self esteem, are we god, how were we brought up to believe ourselves to be. I have the understanding that what we learn in the first seven (7) years of our life, is the foundation of everything we experience thereafter. So the question to ourselves is—what foundation do I have? What have I been taught to be true about myself that isn't? Do I make it true by being in agreement?

The effects of the subtleties and the not so subtleties of women's place in religion and their place with God is similar to the above example. For instance, there is a place in the brain that stores certain symbols and what the meaning of those symbols represent. Example is, the well known cross, the symbol of Jesus being crucified for our sins. I haven't figured out yet which sins they were, the ones after I was born or the ones I supposedly had before I was born, that were just forgiven by baptism or solely by the crucifixion of Jesus. Anyway, what and how we feel about the symbols we see is very subtle indeed since most of the time we are not even aware of seeing them or conscious of how we feel about them. They can cause us to feel guilty about something in particular ie. eating meat on a day of fast, having sexual thoughts, not making the sign of the cross while passing a church, having a great time on Sunday, or Sabbath even though you didn't attend church or synagogue that day.

One may consciously or unconsciously feel guilty of any or all of the rules, rituals, regulations set forth by the religions they have chosen to follow even if just one was broken. I know people who are even afraid to read certain books, see certain movies or talk to certain people because they have been warned against this by the doctrine of their religion. How women are treated in accordance with the chosen religious doctrine is very important here as stated above. Subconsciously one might feel guilty about any or all of it. The crucifixion, for example, can cause you great feelings of guilt for supposedly having another (Jesus) suffer so for your sins. What an affect that could have on your psyche!

If any of this is true and we do indeed have these subtle emotions regarding certain symbols, where did we get them from and how then does it affect our relationship to God and/or our ability to be God in imitating the creative aspect of God? How can one fully realize their potentials of free will, thought and the different outcomes of the various choices made in life based on those same emotions?

Women being ostracized is not new. Even in this day and age women continue to be treated less than men and therefore less than God. Women are still being paid less in wages for the same job. They still, in most cases, work three jobs, that of a mother, home keeper and wage earner. In my observations, in order for women to be accepted into the world of men, they have to act like men. Case in point, the movie G.I. Jane. If anyone saw it, it seems to be about a woman struggling to be treated equal to men. I didn't see it that way. The way I saw it was that there she was, in a man's world, trying to accomplish the same thing the men did by going through the same basic training. She was treated very roughly by both the men and the people in charge. Of course they didn't accept her right away. First she had to show them she was just like them. Rough, tough, could take a beating, could drink down those beers like them, walk like them, talk like them, sleep in their quarters. She shaved her hair like them. Then and only then, did they accept her as one of them. Well, why not? She changed her female qualities to be as they were in order to be accepted. Was she really accepted as a female? I don't think so. Why? Because she wasn't who she was as a female—long hair or short because it suited her, sleeping and living in her own quarters because of her desire for privacy, refusing to be boisterous in bars and drinking beers simply to be accepted. Even in business, until recently, women in executive positions, (if they got there) wore suits like the men did basically acting the male role instead of their inherent selves.

What was proven there !!!—that women can be equal to men? Women are already equal to men but somewhere somehow, there is a need to prove it. I don't think proving it means women need to change themselves and act like men but continue to act like the beautiful people women are with the capacity to create, procreate and recreate. Well, now you might say, oh! but women are treated fairly now, times have changed. Have they? Look at the sexual revolution. Who has to be thin, young, strong and always ready sexually? Women. Do men have to be thin? Pot bellies are expected in men. How many women with pot bellies get picked up, hit on, so to speak? What about weight? Women who are overweight do not get the same treatment as women who are thin.

A Washington TV station did a report regarding the body female on women's health. It discussed the issue of dieting in America and why women in particular felt the need to diet. Most women interviewed stated that they felt unworthy and unwanted if they were overweight. The question I asked myself was, for whom did we need to feel worthy and wanted? The answer was quite clear. Men. It was because of men that we dieted along with the judgments of other women. The dieting is perpetuated by the fact that it is a 40 billion dollar a year business with only about a 3% success rate. The report also cited that teens diet because they wanted to have a boyfriend. If they didn't look like what they perceive the boys or men wanted, then the teens and women developed low self-esteem. They see these ads on TV with long legged woman 5'10 in height. They don't know, however, per that report that the average model is 5'11" and 110 pounds—a body weight below the guidelines for malnutrition. Many women have eating disorders and the dieting is starting at around the age of 10 and 12 years of age. 42% of fourth-grade girls want to be thinner, and 7 million American girls and women are battling potentially life-threatening eating disorders.

How can women perceive or believe themselves to be Gods when they are so programmed to believe otherwise, ie. unworthy, unwanted, sinful and not complete unless there is a man in their life? Yes, we can say women have come a long way but we are not there yet. Women are still the most prejudiced against people in history. Sure there are some who would say they are treated equally by their families but what about in their neighborhood, their town, city, state, country, world. Do we still have to look slim and wear great clothes to feel good about ourselves? Do we still have to look sexy, be sexy, talk sexy and do the things we would rather not do but society says "everybody does" so we should too, in order to be first wanted then kept—I can bring home the bacon, fry it up in the pan and never, never let you forget you're a man—syndrome. What's that??? With all of this, where could God be in us?

Somewhere inside of us there is a creative power, intuitiveness and strength that we don't recognize in ourselves because we have never looked, are discouraged to look at or simply programmed to focus elsewhere. If women were the great Priestesses, Goddesses, Rulers etc. such as Ishtar, Inanna, Nuit, Nefertiti, Mary, mother of Jesus, Mary Magdalene, Cleopatra, Queen Isabelle, Queen Elizabeth I, and many more, the power was there and still is for many women, then we know it must be still there not only for those women but for all women even now. Perhaps if we went deeper into ourselves such as what we are actually made of, we could find the creative powers of God in us after all.

Let's take a quantum leap into quantum mechanics to study the very small of us, the cells, molecules atoms that all things are made up of, including our human bodies men and women alike. Through the study of quantum mechanics, in the Ancient School, I found that in order for an atom to coagulate into molecules, then to mass, they have to have an intention and program. Quantum physics seems to say that it is the observer of the atom or particle that determines what the particles become. I say, if that is so, and I think it is, then we are pretty powerful beings aren't we?

Take the example of Schroedinger's Cat experiment that indicates that if you put a cat in a box and sometime later look in the box to see if the cat is alive or dead, that you will see the cat alive or dead according to your observation. This seems to quite simply mean, according to quantum theory that the observer creates reality according to their expectation. The experiment mentioned here does not separate men from women but includes both. Science tells us that everything is made up of particles. Everything.

Taken from Doug Craigen at http://www.dctech.com/eureka/short-stories/cat.php

> "Two very famous scientists who couldn't agree on the answer were Einstein and Schroedinger. One day Schroedinger explained his opinion to Einstein by talking about his cat. He suggested that you put a cat in a box with a bottle of poison, and the bottle will open and kill the cat at some time that you don't know. Then at some later time is the cat dead or alive? Einstein says that it is one or the other, but we can't know which until we open the box. Schroedinger says that it is neither—the cat is a mixture of dead and alive, and only becomes one or the other when we open the box."

Schroedinger won the 1933 Nobel Prize in physics.

That suggests to me that when you open the box and look in it, it is either dead or alive according to your perception of the contents. Everyone's perception is different. Who is it that gives the intention to a particle to become something, if not you? It's the thinker, the observer of the particle with the thoughts intended. I have had the experiences enough to know this is true for me and if it is true for me, then it must be true for everyone.

I have been taught the process of creating one's day, reality of the day I wish to experience. While I cannot prove my mind and/or my experiential truth, I can certainly share my truths with you regarding that. I have specifically created certain desires and have had them manifested in my reality straight away. I am sure, if you thought about it, you experienced the same thing. You had a thought and next thing there it was in your reality. You probably didn't realize it but you from your mind, created that. The only thing that I know of that can alter the outcome of what you have specifically created are those attitudes, old programs, you know those things that may not give you the permission to have the reality you desire.

Women really need to look into the dynamics of the neuro net in the areas of the brain to find out what attitudes have been attained and retained with regards to ourselves, our past, our environment, our culture, family history, associative memories, etc, and find out who we really are in order to allow the God within us to come forward and be who we really are without the limitations of the patterns of old programs. I have looked and I have learned—Yes, I am a woman, I am a God. As God is becoming, I am becoming. This then is one of the greatest realizations I have come to have. This understanding had been a long time coming but I did finally realize it. It is proven to me every moment of my life simply because I think, so I am and I have a reality produced in which to experience.

Chapter 2

Destiny By Right

Destiny by Right was a hard learned lesson for me. The reason it was so hard was because I hadn't known that I had a limitation as to what I had a right to experience, own, be, love, freedom to express and every other good thing one would want for oneself as destiny.

Having been born in the united states of America under the auspices of being free and having unalienable rights under God, one necessarily assumes that means free by right to whatever one wants in life (within the guidelines of moral code of course). I had no reason to think otherwise until I came to understand, by and through my being a student of the Ramtha School of Enlightenment Ancient School of Wisdom's basic and absolute teaching that we are Gods, creators in personal reality. Somehow though not all my desires or manifestations were realized. If they were, sometimes it didn't last very long in my experiential reality. I was left wondering why reality occurred that way for me? What were my limitations?

How many of us have heard stories of a number of people who won millions of dollars in the lottery, for instance, only to have eventually lost it all and/or ended up in debt?

Columnist Mort Crim article—Keeping It—2004

"Ever wonder what happens to folks who win the lottery? Or even more significantly, what happens to their money? A little digging into the lives of several winners turns up some surprising . . . and disturbing . . . answers And it's clear hitting the lottery jack pot does not necessarily lead to happily ever after. It was just eleven years ago that Suzanne Mullins won more than four million dollars in the Virginia lottery. Today, she not only is broke, she's 154,000. dollars in debt. Hard to believe? Not for Tom Nasta. He's a personal financial planner in Roanoke. Tom says it's not unusual for people to go broke after winning the lottery. He had a client who won $1 million and within seven years, all he had left to show for it was a mobile home. I guess we shouldn't be too surprised. Think of the number of movie stars . . . singers . . . professional athletes . . . who've earned huge fortunes during their careers . . . yet end up penniless or worse, heavily in debt or bankrupt . . . In the final analysis, it's not how much we make that determines wealth. It's how much we're able to keep."

How many have experienced or have heard about people experiencing beautiful events in their lives, only to have it quickly change? Did they really feel worthy of their dreams? Did they fully accept their dreams in their realities or were they somehow sabotaged by their own beliefs about their right to have it? Many people are taught, in religion for example, that you may not get to heaven or serve God as a rich man, as in:

Mark 10:23 And Jesus looked round about, and saith unto his disciples, How hardly shall they that have riches enter into the kingdom of God!

Matthew 6:24 No man can serve two masters: for either he will hate the one, and love the other; or else he will hold to the one, and despise the other. Ye cannot serve God and mammon.

Matthew 19:24 And again I say unto you, It is easier for a camel to go through the eye of a needle, than for a rich man to enter into the kingdom of God.

If one thought they may not get to heaven if they were wealthy, then could it be possible one would unknowingly, through those limited thoughts, sabotage their reality in obtaining and keeping wealth, as an example?

As far as wealth goes and getting into heaven, I have only to look at the wealth of the Vatican, for example. Do we think the Pope may not make it into heaven? He may or may not have personal wealth but it seems to me he is pretty well taken care of. After all, there are starving people all over the world even right outside of the Vatican while a great number of priceless paintings are hanging in the Sistine Chapel building alone not to mention the rest of the buildings laden with gold and such. Go figure! I think that says something. It's the obvious unobvious. It doesn't seem to me that the Pope is particularly worried about fitting through the eye of a needle. He seems to have accepted being richly taken care of.

Another example would be our very own president Bush. He seems to be talking Christian and God. He and his family are a dynasty. Their family has purportedly enormous wealth. In his position as President as well as the purported personal wealth, he too seems to have accepted being richly taken care of. I can't imagine he is too concerned about fitting through the eye of a needle to get into heaven.

Teachings like those above may translate in one's mind as—I don't have a right to have it, I feel guilty about having it, God may not love me or it would be hard getting into heaven, I'm not worthy, we are all sinners, money is the root of all evil and on and on. Would we necessarily be aware that those types of indoctrinations could have significant affects on our abilities to create the kinds of realities that we want to experience?

The many years I have attended Ramtha's school, I learned, first by his teachings and then by experience that I did indeed create my personal reality. I had wonderful and not so wonderful manifestations in my reality of unconscious personal thought as well as in consciously creating certain desires. I hadn't realized what my true belief was in the area of having "rights" to experience those realities.

Ramtha has taught on many occasions too numerous to recount here, that humanity has been subjugated for eons beginning with the creating of these bodies, as they now are, for servitude to the gods of old.

In Ramtha, A Master's Reflection On The History Of Humanity: Part I, *Human Civilization, Origins and Evolution.* Yelm: JZK Publishing, a division of JZK, Inc., 2001.

> (page 187) "You are into your sexuality and you are into your problems, so you have some belief system based upon your emotional body. That is wrongo in the Congo, and if you had used your brains instead of your penises, you would understand that your genetic history traces back to this time in Africa, the house of the breath of life. And who was the scientist, the head of that? Mammy. That is where it goes back to, in Africa, the cradle of civilization. Where were her children taken? To the land between the Tigris and Euphrates Rivers. They were taken all over the world. They would become the new slave labor of the Gods."

> (page190) "And it took over a hundred and twenty years to develop the perfect DNA strand that would then allow an entity who looked like the Gods, who had a large brain—They inherited the yellow brain. They would have all of the abilities. They would be as tall. They would be as beautiful but they would be servants."

> (page 191) "So 450,000 years ago, the Gods came here and there were already primitive human beings evolving and evolving to make known the unknown, and they created them as a remarkable jump-start on evolution. They gave those who weren't prepared for it the mechanisms to be able to think and be, consider, and contemplate complex problems. So they made them into slaves and they made them work in the mines, mine gold as one great mining."

In addition to Ramtha's teaching, Zecharia Sitchin confirms these teachings through his work as an esteemed translator and writer. Zecharia Sitchin was born in Russia and raised in Palestine, where he acquired a profound knowledge of modern and ancient Hebrew, other Semitic and European languages, the Old Testament, and the history and archeology of the Near East. He is one of the few scholars who is able to read and understand Sumerian. Sitchin attended and graduated from the University of London, majoring in economic history. He has been a leading journalist and editor in Israel for many years.

Confirmation comes in some of his writings that the Annunaki (the Gods) using in-vitro fertilization techniques and genetic manipulation created "primitive workers" to mine for gold because the work was so hard that the gods no longer wanted to do it. He talks about the African mines. It appears that the Annunaki mutinied. One of the gods Enki suggested creating primitive workers through genetic manipulation. Assuming this is the case, then I conclude that the gods at that time, already had the knowledge to alter the DNA of a certain species of man, possibly homo sapiens. They came out of Africa. This I believe to be the missing link.

In addition, I read in Discover, Vol. 25 No. 12. that according to the work done with DNA at the University of Arizona, the chromosomes studied showed that "Adam" lived in Africa around 50,000 years ago along with "Eve".

There are many other sources that have clearly established the servitude of men and in particular women. When one is literally bred for servitude how does your genetics deal with your "rights". Do you really have any? What do you allow yourself? Do you accept being a co-creator with God as a God? Can you really do anything in your life that isn't for the act of survival but solely because you just wanted to and that was OK without compromising?

The information set forth here clearly shows us that we also have the DNA of the gods and all that that implies. We have the advanced DNA of the gods of old. DNA that has the potential of great power. That's very good news, however, we all too often compromise ourselves, our wants, our needs, loves, joy, family and friends because that is the only way to survive. Most people will work at a job that they really don't want to do, or even enjoy doing, for 40 or more hours a week. This leaves little time for family, friends, entertainment, hobbies, not to mention just time for recreation (re-creation, the time to re-create anew) in addition to the very important sleep time, when according to studies your body has a chance to heal itself from the day's use and in some cases abuse.

> "WB&A Market Research conducted the 2001 Sleep in America poll by telephone for the National Sleep Foundation with a random sample of 1004 adults at least 18 years of age . . . Sleep in America Poll Executive Summary—Titled : LESS FUN, LESS SLEEP, MORE WORK

AN AMERICAN PORTRAIT National Sleep Foundation
Poll Shows Americans Living to Work, Not Working to Live;
Foundation Urges Americans to 'Make Time For Sleep' . . .
"Those who report the following medical conditions are
most likely to experience a sleep problem: depression(83%),
nighttime heartburn (82%), diabetes (81%), cancer (79%),
hypertension(79%), heart disease (78%) and/or arthritis
(76%). More than one-third of adults (38%) say they snore
frequently, a problem reported more by males than females
(45% vs. 30%)"

We, this includes me, do all this for the sake of a paycheck so we
can buy food, take care of our families, provide shelter and some
finer things in life. I believe this too is an act of subtle inner sense
of servitude. We have a tendency to forget about our dreams and
often regret and resent the cause of our forgetfulness. I came to
realize that unless you are doing something you really want to do,
love to do and are happy at doing, then it is a compromise of life. I
came to realize that we do this because it is inherently in our genes
as well as, in some instances, cultural idealistic views together with
other sources as well. We get the reward of getting what we need in
return. If we didn't do that, well, we may not get our needs met. We
were not bred to be gods, creators with the God source nor were we
to be given the knowledge of our inherent creative abilities.

It is not intended to say that we should not work at all unless it is
something we love to do, for it is also important to understand that
one must be honorable and take care of our responsibilities to
families and communities, if for nothing else, for the sake of order
and well being, even while we are striving to meet our goals. The
important thing here is that we do set goals of those dreams we wish
to experience, knowing that it is our inherent right to realize those
dreams while, in the meantime, do whatever is necessary to take
care of whatever we have made obligation to careful not to make
frivolous obligations.

One can see in the societies around the world, rights are given
and rights are taken away. The ones in power decide your future.
It's funny because there are so few of them and a lot more of us.
That begs the question why with so few in power and so many not,
why the few are able to over power the many? We do after all, have
the same brain mass and body mass. In those respects, humans

were created equal. So what's the difference? I think it is because we don't exercise our personal power within all of us to create for ourselves. Humanity has a tendency to have others do it or are too tired surviving to think about it or we just don't think we can or have the right to.

In the study of the areas of the brain, I was taught that the subconscious mind is the gateway to God the source, aka, infinite unknown, point zero etc. and has direct and indirect access to the frontal lobe where what you image there, creates out here in your reality. We all have access to the same thing by and through our own brains. That being the case and according to science, quantum physics, as noted in the beginning writing here, it's the observer who creates the reality by the act of observation. There really is no difference with the exception of what we are taught to believe is true vs what we experience to be true, the quality of our education and what has been for eons the indoctrination. Is or has servitude been the indoctrination instead of personal power and personal responsibility? Is or has victimization been the indoctrination instead of personal power and personal responsibility? Is or has compromise been the way instead of personal power? Does God really judge what we do or have done or is it our personality, ego, image that judges ourselves according to what we have been indoctrinated to believe?

Women in particular have been subjugated and made to feel less than even to this day in many places around the world (again as noted in the beginning writing here). Just take a look at the most recent events in Afghanistan, Iraq, anywhere a woman gets paid less for doing the same job as a man, taking double duty with holding down a job and caring for husband, family etc. While this is certainly changing, it still remains for the most part that women have an unworthiness aspect to them. If that were not so, most women wouldn't be so concerned about their figures, age, etc. Just look at the numbers of plastic surgeries women have.

In the following Press Release titled:

> 6.6 Million Americans Get A Nip, Tuck, And Lift With Cosmetic Plastic Surgery In 2002 American Society of Plastic Surgeons Reports 2002 Statistics For Immediate Release: April 15, 2003

Gender Women represent the majority of patients when it comes to cosmetic plastic surgery. More than 5.6 million women (85 percent) and nearly 1 million men (15 percent) had cosmetic plastic surgery in 2002. The top five surgical cosmetic procedures for women in 2002 were breast augmentation (236,888), liposuction (230,079), nose reshaping (209,123),eyelid surgery (186,522) and facelift (105,850). This is the first time in 10 years that breast augmentation was the most popular cosmetic plastic surgery procedure. The top five non-surgical cosmetic procedures for women were Botox® injection (991,114), chemical peel (771,542), microdermabrasion(771,314), sclerotherapy (495,610) and laser hair removal (484,787). The top five surgical cosmetic procedures for men in 2002 were nose reshaping (145,204), liposuction (52,797), eyelid surgery (44,150), hair transplantation (26,501) and ear surgery (21,316). The top five non-surgical cosmetic procedures for men were chemical peel (148,798), Botox® injection(132,396), microdermabrasion (129,598), laser hair removal (102,753) and collagen injection (41,193).

Take note that the number of women having some sort of correction is far greater than that of men. There is clearly also a great interest in teenagers using plastic surgery for reasons of self-esteem as the below article indicates:

Facial Plastic Surgery Today—A newsletter of the American Academy of Facial Plastic and Reconstruction Surgeries—Third Quarter 2001, Vol. 15,No. 3—Teens turn to facial plastic surgery to improve self-esteem. "The teenage years are replete with rapid changes physically and mentally as a child tries to forge his or her own path into young adulthood. On top of issues of independence, there are concerns about acceptance by peers and anxiety about appearance. Why are teenagers seeking facial plastic surgery and is it right for my teen?"

Who would women be unworthy to? Who would men be unworthy to? Teenagers? In comparison to what or who? What rights do we conclude to have when we may have these inner feelings that say we should look a certain way, act a certain way, do certain things, say certain things, follow certain rituals, live by rules made up by interpretations of writings translated long ago, which may not even be correct, in order to experience the reality of our dreams?

All beings have these God inherent rights. We can use our own brains as observers and creators of personal reality. I personally don't believe God restricted happiness with the fulfillment of one's dreams to only those that are beautiful, skinny, poor, suffering, men of servitude but to any of us regardless without restriction. We only need to know our own thinking to change the course of our lives.

Let us look at the role religion has had in the lives of all of us. It really doesn't matter which religion, they all accomplish the same thing. Subjugation. You are a servant to God, you can be punished by God, you are unworthy next to God, almost anything you enjoy is against God's will, and on and on. One has to wonder what ever happened to free will, the God given free will we were supposed to have? Where does free will ever fit in with regard to religion? Do we really have free will or do we just think we do?? Free will is very pertinent with respect to our rights because if we don't intrinsically know we have the right to experience anything we choose, then we can't use our will freely.

Is there a stigma to the long subjugation and servitude women have experienced and many still feel? Do women truly feel an intrinsic right to freely accept all the manifestations of their dreams? Do all men? Many men also experience subjugation and servitude, having come from the same seeds long ago being bred for service. The men may unknowingly sabotage their dreams for some of the same reasons as stated here. I am by no means excluding men.

Having said all that, it may be true all of humanity may not be indoctrinated by servitude or victimization and certainly do allow all life has to offer into their reality but I think for the most part we are indoctrinated and its very very subtle. For me it was so subtle that it took me a long time and who knows how many lifetimes to come to the understanding that if God has a direct line to your frontal lobe via the subconscious and whatever you image there, will or can be realized in your reality, the image in the frontal lobe is not judged by God, the only one judging us is us, then we need to look at what judgement, belief, indoctrination we have which would limit our very own desires from manifesting or perhaps greatly diminish it. Do I really have the right to experience anything I choose in my reality? The answer can be nothing else but yes!!! Yes!!! Yes!!!

We are the observer and as such, if what we observe is colored by our own belief and/or indoctrinations, it would necessarily limit our reality to only that perception or view. If God will give us anything then who's not allowing it? According to quantum physics and the teaching as I understand them from Ramtha, it is the observer we are that whatever we observe we experience in reality. We do indeed affect the quantum field and it acts accordingly.

Referring to Lynne McTaggart's book, The Field, where she suggests that other scientists such as, Walter Schempp, mathemetics professor University of Siegen, Germany, Dr. Edgar Mitchell, astronaut and founder of the Institute of Noetic Sciences in 1972, Peter Marcer, British physicist, have indicated a potential that perception was more at the level of matter, the quantum particle more at the level of point zero, the void. The unseen. They couldn't see objects but received wave frequency information. But who gives the particles the information as to which potential to become. It seems to me, that as the observers of reality, we do.

Mc Taggart also refers to Wilhelm Roentgen, recipient of Nobel Prize in physics 1901, accidentally discovering that rays of certain frequency produced pictures of hard structures of the body. And as suggested by Karl Pribram, noted physicist, that the art of seeing, our perception, observation, if you will, is transforming time and space. That time and space is created on our retinas.

In conclusion, it seems according to quantum scientists, it is that the physical world exists in a solid state so long as we observed it, were involved in it. This really has been my experience and perhaps yours. Perhaps you were dreaming about something, for a short time or long time, you were involved in those dreams, perhaps envisioning yourself, imagining, daydreaming, so to speak, you even forgot where you were or what you were doing. One day—lo and behold—you were experiencing those dreams. You may not have connected the two but through quantum physics one can surmise that we are indeed creators as God, manipulators of the quantum field and because of that we can realize any desire we choose. Instead of being the force that consciously creates what I choose, I have, we all have been creating the attitudes and thoughts we were conscious of as well as those we are unconscious of. We are fully within our right to ask and receive. I did find out I was the only one limiting my dreams and am now searching out those hidden agendas, beliefs, judgments, indoctrinations, in the corners of my brain which only hamper my quality of life and negate my dreams.

Is this then what Jesus meant when he said as quoted in: Jung And The Lost Gospels by Stephan A. Hoeller, The Gospel of Thomas saying #67:

> "He who knows the all but fails to have self-knowledge lacks everything."

I have heard many many times a saying—". . . . the truth shall set you free." For me it means the truth about me. The more truth, the freer I am in my mind to realize any dream I have the capacity to dream.

Chapter 3

Destiny by Choice

Who do I want to be? Where do I want to go? What would I like to experience? With whom shall I share my life? These are some of the many questions, without limit, one could ask oneself but what are the answers? McTaggart refers to Stuart Hameroff, an anesthesiologist from University of Arizona and his idea indicating from his work with microtubules—that electrons glide easily along light pipes without getting entangled in their environment. concluding the idea that they can remain in a quantum state, a condition of all possible states, allowing the brain to choose among them, a plausible explanation for free will. In addition, every moment, our brains are making quantum choices taking potential states and making them actual ones.

When the smoke is cleared the question remains where do I go from here? Now that I know I can create anything, what will it be?—That perhaps is the hardest question most of us can ask ourselves. We are only limited by our own understanding and knowledge base. What we don't know exists, we can't dream about. The importance of knowledge, therefore, is clearly seen. We don't know what we don't know!

Through our many years of conventional schooling, we are taught many established versions of history. Unless we did the actual research or were there at the time, would we know for sure history was as stated in the history books? I heard it said somewhere that those in power, rewrite history. What about science? Unless we actually did all the experimentation or research in all the sciences, would we truly know that what we were being taught or told is indeed fact?

Of course, we know that it wouldn't be practical or possible to research everything. There are others who do it. Others who then become the authority on those particular subjects. In that, however, there is significant risk in taking another's word for it. There could be many reasons individual people or groups of people would give you less than the truth about any subject. Scientists may be afraid for example, to offer true scientific research results if they were afraid they wouldn't get the grants necessary to continue their work. Also ego plays a huge role. One may be convinced to offer altered information for advancement of their own ego or bank account, power as well as countless other reasons.

Just look at the conflicting information regarding humanity's true origin. Archeological finds prove one thing while some history books say another. Look at the conflicting information regarding UFO's—information, misinformation and the like. It becomes our job to sift through all of this to build on our experiential base as well as knowledge base in order to even begin to think about the great question, where do I go from here? If we have a small base, we can only create small realities, if we have a great base, well then we can expand greatly our realities. These may even include something as extraordinary as inter-dimensional travel. Time travel. Turning water into wine. Look at all the possibilities. You know, when we buy certain products, they usually come with an instruction manual regarding how to use the product along with the products' uses and capabilities. Unfortunately, when we are born, we don't come with instructions nor are we given any, on why we have brains or how to use our brains to its' full potential. I understand that we only use about 1/10th of our brain mass. Why not the rest? What is the rest of our brain for? What is our brain capable of achieving? If we knew that, what grandness can we achieve? We are only limited by our knowledge base.

Referring to our brains, making quantum choices, if I didn't take the time to learn about the quantum field, I would have never known about the unlimited potentials I can create from for experiential reality. I took the responsibility to gain as much information as I could. I wasn't too stuck in conventional ideas, status quo history, status quo science. I took the leap into the worlds studied and researched by many. I sorted them out and gained great knowledge and wisdom because I experienced some of the things I learned about. Now I have great truths added to life. This is how I evolve my mind and not stagnate in life. It is not only a question of obtaining wealth or success but evolving out of the stagnation of the mundane.

You know the same old same old. I got bored with that. I began to go outside of the conventional. That was how I began listening to Ramtha's teachings. There was controversy as to whether Ramtha was Ramtha or JZ Knight, who channels him, was really the one and who was who. To me that never mattered because the information was so mind grabbing that I couldn't learn enough or get enough information offered. Because I made that choice, my life changed. I learned what some of my limitations were. I had greater experiences. This is how I know what I learned was truth.

In Ken Wilber's book The Spectrum of Consciousness, page 189, it states:

> "In a similar vein, Bernard Lonergan, in his monumental study on insight and understanding, stressed one major point: Thoroughly understand what it is to understand, and not only will you understand the broad lines of all there is to be understood but also you will possess a fixed base, an invariant pattern, opening upon all further developments of understanding. 39."

I was able to make different choices because I had a greater knowledge base in which to choose from.

Those different choices produce a different destiny. I am sure all people have seen the results of making a certain choice and how that choice created a reality, wonderful or not. It really doesn't matter what your choices are, they will unfold a certain destiny. Like it or not here it comes.

We really need to be vigilant in our own belief systems, thinking processes, actions and inactions. We want to be somewhat sure we don't miss the moment. Missing the moment is when we say—I should have, could have and so on, which brings me to the point of living our past over and over again. I have learned that we only do that because we constantly think about the past. That is the only thing our brain thinks about because that is all we know. What we don't now know but somehow learn about, is the future. It makes sense, that if we do indeed create our realities by our attitudes and thoughts, then we would need new thoughts and changed attitudes to realize new realities to be experienced.

Again in Ken Wilber's book The Spectrum of Consciousness page 123 he quotes Emerson (from "Self-reliance"):

> "These roses under my window make no reference to former roses or to better ones; they are for what they are; they exist with God today. There is no time for them. There is simply the rose; it is perfect in every moment of its existence . . . But man postpones or remembers; *he does not live in the present,* but with reverted eye laments the past, or, heedless of the riches that surround him, stands on tiptoe to foresee the future. He cannot be happy and strong until he too lives with nature in the present, above time." Emphasis added.

The only way I know of to get out of past thinking is to pay attention to what I am doing now. This, along with meditation, can bring you to a place outside of your present thinking to a place, we can readily tap into, where the new thoughts exist. For me that is the Kingdom of Heaven, the void, point zero, the source. It makes sense to me especially with respect my experiences in doing just that, meditating, contemplation and allowing the answers or knowledge to flow. It may not always come the way you may have imagined it to come to you but that would be limited thinking again. People, places, things, times and events will come into your reality to suit the intent and purpose. How do I know? Been there, done that and still do have these types of experiences.

> Matthew 7:7—"Ask and it will be given to you; seek and you will find; knock and the door will be opened to you."

In addition, one really needs to ask oneself how they truly feel about any one thing. Listen to your thoughts—you know, those other thoughts, the ones that you think while you are saying something else. Those are the thoughts that are very important. Listen to them, they will tell you who you are and what you really believe. If none of those thoughts suit you, you can change them just by not allowing them to permeate your mind and immediately put a new better thought in their stead.

As I said earlier, situations don't always happen that make us happy. In fact, most of us have thoughts which don't always make us happy, thoughts we would rather not think about. In those cases one simply chases the thought away, meaning to not dwell on it or one invokes the act of forgiving oneself for the thought(s). That is, in my understanding what forgiveness is all about. It cleans the slate, so to speak which allows us to move on.

Author: A Course In Miracles Course on Forgiveness Based on Christianity, Eastern Philosophy

"I can elect to change all thoughts that hurt."

In addition situations or results may take some time to be realized. After we have stood guard over our thoughts and beliefs, we can rest assured that our efforts won't go unrealized. The only one that can stop their realization is our change of mind. As long as we have intent and purpose, goals if you will, then sooner or later it happens, just the way we thought it.

> "Depend on it. God's work, done in God's way, will never lack God's supply. He is too wise a God to frustrate His purposes for lack of funds, and He can just as easily supply them ahead of time as afterwards, and He much prefers doing so."—J. Hudson Taylor (China Inland Mission) 1832-1905.

I am happy to say that the cutting edge of science, quantum science in particular, verifies and continues establishing the truths concerning what I have written here.

There is a wonderful movie titled "What The (bleep) Do We Know? It has already won numerous awards. The title is apt. We won't know what the (bleep) we don't know until we find out what we don't know. This is quite a journey, one I am still on. I have come a long way, there is still more to do and there is still more to go. Nonetheless, I am willing to continue working on it.

Knowledge is everything. When you have it and don't doubt your possibilities, you can do anything and have anything.

> Matthew 21:19-22
>
> *19* And when he saw a fig tree in the way, he came to it, and found nothing thereon, but leaves only, and said unto it, Let no fruit grow on thee henceforward for ever. And presently the fig tree withered away.
>
> *20* And when the disciples saw *it,* they marveled, saying, How soon is the fig tree withered away!
>
> *21* Jesus answered and said unto them, Verily I say unto you, If ye have faith, and doubt not, ye shall not only do this which is done to the fig tree, but also if ye shall say unto this mountain, Be thou removed, and be thou cast into the sea; it shall be done.
>
> *22* And all things, whatsoever ye shall ask in prayer, believing, ye shall receive.

According to science, as noted herein, who is doing the asking? It suggests the observer, through thoughts, perception and belief. The quantum field, the God source, the void will give you anything.

Knowledge is POWER. The CHOICE is ours!

Chapter 4

Destiny's Time Line

So what is our destiny going to be? Can we change it? I have been taught by Ramtha that we most certainly can change it and do with every thought we have. If, however, we have the same old thoughts, then we have the same destiny we started with unfolding in our lives.

Time lines are an interesting subject. Most everyone has heard the expression used but few know what it really is about—what it really means.

All that I wrote on these pages, gives the reader ideas and knowledge which perhaps they didn't have before. For some, these ideas might be considered way out of the box of the norm. I hope that is true because to be out of the box means one has changed or will change their destiny's time line. Can it be proven? Probably not unless you were such an aware entity that you knew what your destiny was and when it changed. But, how would you prove it? Personal experience and truth I don't think, can ever be proven to someone else, although you can ask, who is there I would need to prove it to?

We all have a time line from point A to point B. Straight as an arrow. Assuming we continue on the same path day in and day out, very little will pivot you away from the course set. All our emotions have some sort of an affect on our daily lives and it is those very same emotions that can catapult us to a different time line or remain on the same. Remember the choice has always been ours. We are the ones who have the control of how we perceive things or how we re-act to things emotionally. All of that can be changed, if we choose to and that includes changing our destiny's time line.

How does it happen you ask. How can it happen you may ask. Well, again, if we turn to science we may find the answers.

There is no past, or future. We only have now, the moment in what we call time in which we actively participate, meaning experiencing, feeling. There is a presentation of science given by Brian Green, Columbia University, shown on Nova many many times, maybe you saw it, entitled "The Elegant Universe". It talked about what science has come to suspect and know about the universe, the nature of life, quantum field, time and space. It clearly showed to me the science of all that I wrote here with regards to what the possibilities of potentials are for a greater more expansive life irrespective of time, space etc. What we can do and experience is virtually limitless.

It seems, according to Brian Green's presentation, we could be in two places at once, what a trip that would be. In addition, go backwards in time or forwards in time. Whatever you can conceive of in thought outside the box of the "norm". Is it easy? Could be!!!!! How difficult do we want to make it??? My teacher Ramtha, has taught this to his students for many years. Science is just now catching up.

If you think about the past, where is the past you are thinking about? When you think about the future, where is the future you are thinking about? When you are busy thinking about either past or future, you are bringing either to the now moment. You are living the past or present in that now moment. If you are past thinking, what happened to the awareness of the now moment of your surroundings, of the song you're enjoying or the book you thought you were reading or the dreams you were dreaming?

Now if that is the case, than the time line is nothing more than the path we follow in our experiential reality based on the patterns of our thoughts unfolding holographically. If we are experiencing our physical senses, walking, talking etc., with the element of time passing by, we can surmise we are on our time line. As we move through time we are first born, we move on in our lives experiencing, then we continue moving on and die. Point A to point B. But, is that set in stone? Could we actually change the outcome of our destiny? Why is it that everyone has a different life span? How is that decided?? Who decides it??? We decide it and we decide it based on our emotions, opinions, knowledge and will. Isn't it interesting that many times you might hear someone saying to some else "do you have the will to live?". If on some level one didn't know the importance of that question, no one would ever have asked it. It is asked, because it matters if someone has a will to do something or not, including living or dying.

An example being this. The well known "placebo affect". Did you believe you were taking medication or did you not know! What you believed to be so, i.e. medication would help you heal, it did and consequently you lived a longer happier life even though you were taking the "placebo". In addition, as in the old story roughly as follows: a doctor sends a diagnosis to one patient saying that they would be well soon. He then sends another patient the news of their impending demise within 6 mos. By mistake he sends the wrong message to the wrong patient. The well one dies withing 6 mos. and the other lives. Would you say their respective time lines were changed because of what they believed to be so? Would this then show that time lines can be altered by our own thoughts?

What if you become deathly ill and you feel there is no hope, nobody, not even the medical profession would be able to help you, you become so desperate that you are willing now to do anything, try anything so you do. A friend comes to you and says, you know, I found this wonderful woman in Mexico who has this wonderful herb. It has worked wonders for many people with the same condition as yours. Would you like to take a trip to meet this person to see what can be done for you? Well, at this point, you have two choices, one is certain death, the other is possibility of continued life. Now you choose. Your choice will be based on your attitudes about such things, your experiences as well as your associations, your belief systems and how you have been indoctrinated in your life. OK, so you choose to not go. Now you kick the proverbial bucket. Who is to blame??? You stayed the course—point A to point B. You couldn't get out of the box. Make a change. Your time line stayed the course.

Well now, suppose you decided to take the chance, realizing you had nothing to lose as you were already deathly ill. You tell your friend to make the arrangements. You see the lady with the herbs and she is able to help you heal so you become well. You may even attend a school such as Ramtha's where you are taught processes of self-healing. You get to live another however many years. My question is, could you have conceivably changed your destiny's time line just by making a different choice? I would answer yes. You chose to take herbs or attend a school engaging in self-healing techniques.

Too many times, we stay the course. We hold onto the old patterns. We refuse, adamantly I might add, to learn anything new, do anything different, try something new. If that is the case, then how could your life's course change? One has to be a willing participant in life. Someone said—life happens to you when you are busy living it—. I believe that to be true. By living it, I'm not talking about the same old programs the ones in our heads or the ones on the TV but living life complete with the new, sometimes out of the box opportunities. This doesn't mean to be sooo far out as to put yourself in danger. This is not what I mean. One always has to discern what would best be safe for them, after all one wouldn't want to die—prematurely—(see what I mean) before one's time is up. The mere fact that someone takes unnecessary chances tells you something about the character make-up of that person. Unless that changes, that person has written their own destiny to an interesting conclusion.

In the book "Molecules of Emotions—Why You Feel The Way You Feel by Candace B. Pert, tells us how your mind, spirit and emotions are unified within your physical body. Dr. Bruce Lipton, noted cellular biologist and acclaimed speaker, scientist and lecturer, also shows us how our emotions and thoughts affect every cell in the body. He's brilliant.

Changing the way we think along with the will and the decision to heal oneself or change your lifestyle, if necessary, in addition to self realizations produce different time lines. Changing the course of your life has the possible potentiality of extending it or shortening it.

Would it then be our respective choices, as related to the types of beliefs and thoughts we have, that can change our time lines of destiny. What if all were given the opportunity to attend a school, such as Ramtha's, where you were given such lofty knowledge that your reality expanded greatly to where you were able to change time lines inter—dimensionally? Wouldn't that be the catch all!!! You can. It's available to everyone all over the world.

Before such a choice can be made, one would have to be made aware of such a possibility. You would have to be given the knowledge of the existence of potentials other than the limited potentials we have had. This is one of the reasons I decided to share my experience and knowledge with others. I desired to make others aware of the extraordinary lives just waiting to be lived, if we only allowed ourselves, and I might add others, to live them. We have a way of limiting others from experiencing all they can be because we tend to be possessive people and many rarely allow, not only themselves, but family, friends and others as well to make changes, choices because they're afraid of losing them to something else.

I know I have experienced that. We get jealous, lonely, resentful and regretful along with a host of other emotions. These again are only old emotions we hold onto because we are not aware of anything other. When we begin to feel, truly feel secure with ourselves that we are truly God's creating our realities who can change anything at any time, then we have no need to suffer through those old emotions. We only have to change them into something greater a greater potential. It could be easy, it could be hard. What do you say???

This journey is a challenging journey for me but a journey I never intend to stop taking. My mom used to say to me "Louise, when are you going to graduate from this school"? My response was "Hopefully never". The reality I have come to understand is that every time we can evolve an old emotion, it's a graduation because it is then that as a student graduating from college, I begin a new life on a new path with new experiences to a new destiny. So be it!!!!!

References Used

Zecharia Sitchin—referencing—The Earth Chronicles

Discover Magazine—referencing—Vol. 25 No. 12

Lynne Mc Taggart, author—referencing—The Field

The Golden Thread June/July, 2001 referencing—The Bloodline of the Holy Grail by Sir Laurence Gardner

Candace B. Per, author—referencing—Molecules of Emotions

Dr. Bruce Lipton Ph.D.—www.brucelipton.com

Newsletter American Acadeny of Facial Plastic and Reconstruction Surgeries Third Quarter 2001, Vol. 15, No. 3

National Sleep Foundation, Washington, DC 20005—2001 Sleep in America poll

Brian Green, Columbia University, "The Elegant Universe"

Movie: What The (Bleep) Do We Know!!!!

G. I. Jane, 1997